Daily Thoughts
from
Samuel Rutherford

Daily Thoughts
from
Samuel Rutherford

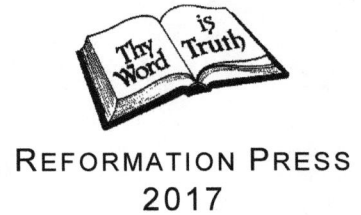

REFORMATION PRESS
2017

British Library Cataloguing in Publication Data
ISBN 978-1-912042-02-9

© Reformation Press 2017

Originally published in 1897 as
*Daily Thoughts for a Year from the
Letters of Samuel Rutherford*

Published by Reformation Press
11 Churchill Drive, Stornoway
Isle of Lewis, Scotland HS1 2NP
www.reformationpress.co.uk

Also available as a Kindle e-book
ISBN 978-1-872556-03-6

Printed by www.lulu.com

All rights reserved. No part of this publication may be reproduced, stored in a retrieval system, or transmitted, in any form or by any means, without the prior permission in writing of Reformation Press, or as expressly permitted by law, by licence, or under terms agreed with the appropriate reprographic rights organisation.

Contents

Introduction	7
January	9
February	16
March	23
April	30
May	37
June	45
July	52
August	62
September	70
October	77
November	85
December	92

Introduction

Samuel Rutherford's *Letters* are widely known and scarcely need an introduction. Those less familiar with them may find a selection of quotations like this the easiest way to begin. The focus on key phrases means that this volume will also be welcomed where the letters are already well loved.

The *Letters of Samuel Rutherford* were first published in 1662 as *Joshua Redivivus*—the original Latin title meaning 'Joshua lives again'. The letters have been highly esteemed in every generation, from Rutherford's own time onwards. Principal John Macleod described them as 'the most remarkable series of devotional letters that the literature of the Reformed Church can show'. C. H. Spurgeon said of them, 'What a wealth of spiritual ravishment we have here! Rutherford is beyond all praise of men. Like a strong-winged eagle he soars into the highest heaven and with unblenched eye he looks into the mystery of love divine ... let the world know that Spurgeon held Rutherford's *Letters* to be the nearest thing to inspiration which can be found in all the writings of men ... none penetrated further into the innermost heart of holy fellowship with Jesus.' Richard Baxter commented in a similar vein, 'Hold off the Bible, such a book a Mr. Rutherford's *Letters*, the world never saw the like.'

It has been frequently observed that, in the providence of God, three hundred and sixty five letters have survived and been collected together. This means that it is possible to read one on each day of the year. The present volume offers one or two thoughts for each day—these can be considered carefully and savoured through meditation. The punctuation has been changed to current norms. Rutherford used Scots words and phrases extensively. Explanations of these are given in brackets.

It is the hope of the publisher that these extracts will be of spiritual benefit and will encourage the reader to study the full text of the incomparable *Letters*.

The Publisher
Stornoway
October 2017

> Every day we may see some new thing in Christ. His love has neither brim nor bottom. How blessed are we to enjoy this invaluable treasure, the love of Christ—or rather, allow ourselves to be mastered and subdued in his love, so that Christ is our all, and all other things are nothing.
>
> *Samuel Rutherford*

January

JANUARY 1

He is unchangeable, and the same this year that he was the former year.
Letter 19

JANUARY 2

He becomes caution [security, surety] to his Father for all such as resolve and promise to serve him.
Letter 1

JANUARY 3

Courage! Up your heart! When ye do tire, he will bear both you and your burden (Psalm 55:22).
Letter 2

JANUARY 4

Herein shall ye have comfort, that he who seeth perfectly through all your evils, and knoweth the frame and constitution of your nature, and what is most healthful for your soul, holdeth every cup of affliction to your head with his own gracious hand.
Letter 3

JANUARY

JANUARY 5

After God's highest and fullest tide, that the sea of trouble is gone over the souls of his children, then comes the gracious long-hoped-for ebbing and drying up of the waters.
Letter 12

JANUARY 6

The Lord hath told you what ye should be doing till he come.
Letter 4

JANUARY 7

Go wheresoever ye will, if your Lord go with you, ye are at home.
Letter 5

JANUARY 8

Here is your Father's testament. Read it; in it he hath left to you remission of sins, and life everlasting.
Letter 7

JANUARY 9

Welcome, welcome, cross of Christ, if Christ be with it.
Letter 8

JANUARY 10

I pray you, be humble and believe.
Letter 9

JANUARY

JANUARY 11

All God's plants, set [planted] by his own hand, thrive well.
Letter 10

JANUARY 12

Whether God come to his children with a rod or a crown, if he come himself with it, it is well.
Letter 11

JANUARY 13

Pray, and be content with his will; God hath a council-house [assembly house] in heaven, and the end will be mercy unto you.
Letter 26

JANUARY 14

He is worthy to be suffered for, not only to blows [receiving blows], but also to blood [shedding blood].
Letter 16

JANUARY 15

Tribulations and temptations will almost loosen us to the root; and yet without tribulations and temptations, we can no more grow than herbs or corn without rain.
Letter 22
He shall take your part, and then you are strong enough.
Letter 15

JANUARY

JANUARY 16

Be content to wade through the waters betwixt you and glory with him, holding his hand fast, for he knoweth all the fords.
Letter 19

JANUARY 17

It were best that we were on Christ's side of it, for his enemies will get only the stalks to keep, as the proverb is.
Letter 17

JANUARY 18

Have your eyes upon none but the Lord of armies, and the Lord shall either let you see what you long to see, or then else fulfil your joy more abundantly another way.
Letter 24

JANUARY 19

Thrice fools are we, who, like newborn princes weeping in the cradle, know not that there is a kingdom before them.
Letter 20

JANUARY 20

It is enough that the Lord hath promised you great things, only let the time of bestowing them be in his

JANUARY

own carving [design]. ... Our love to him should begin on earth, as it shall be in heaven.
Letter 21

JANUARY 21

They are not worthy of Jesus, who will not take a blow for their Master's sake.
Letter 27

Look for crosses [expect tribulations], and while it is fair weather, mend the sails of the ship.
Letter 30

JANUARY 22

Our fair morning is at hand, the day star is near the rising, and we are not many miles from home. What matters ill entertainment in the smoky inns of this miserable life? We are not to stay here, and we will be dearly welcome to him whom we go to.
Letter 26

JANUARY 23

Hold you by his blessed word, and sin not.
Letter 13

JANUARY 24

Hope and believe that the Lord will gather in his loose sheaves among you to his barn.
Letter 18

JANUARY

JANUARY 25

Jesus will make a road, and come and fetch home the captive.
Letter 29

It is more to you to win heaven, being ships of greater burden, and in the main sea [open ocean], than for little vessels, that are not so much in the mercy and reverence [control] of the storms, because they may come quietly to their port by launching alongst [sailing along] the coast.
Letter 30

JANUARY 26

Try what is the taste of the Lord's cup and drink with God's blessing, that ye may grow thereby.
Letter 35

JANUARY 27

The government is upon his shoulders, and he dow [can] bear us all well enough.
Letter 32

JANUARY 28

I think love hath broad shoulders and will bear many things.
Letter 34

JANUARY

JANUARY 29

I trust in God that the Lord, who knit us together, shall keep us together.
Letter 34

JANUARY 30

Ye are a child of the house, and joy is laid up for you.
Letter 37

JANUARY 31

Our Lord hath done all this to see if we will believe and not give over.
Letter 38

February

FEBRUARY 1

His love to you will not grow sour, nor wear out of date.
Letter 39

Good cause have we to wonder at his love.
Letter 14

FEBRUARY 2

God commandeth you now to believe and cast anchor in the dark night.
Letter 39

FEBRUARY 3

I seek no other thing but that my Lord may be honoured by me.
Letter 40

FEBRUARY 4

Fear not, Christ will not cast water upon your smoking coal, and then who else dare do it if he say nay?
Letter 48

FEBRUARY

FEBRUARY 5

If the devil and Zion's enemies strike a hole in that armour, let our Lord see to that. Let us put it on, and stand.
Letter 41

FEBRUARY 6

I wonder many times that ever a child of God should have a sad heart, considering what their Lord is preparing for them.
Letter 41

FEBRUARY 7

The Lord send us to the shore out of all the storms, with our silly [frail and pitiful] souls sound and whole with us.
Letter 44

FEBRUARY 8

It were good that we should knock and rap at our Lord's door. We may not tire to knock oftener than twice or thrice. He knoweth the knock of his friends.
Letter 46

FEBRUARY 9

I adore and kiss the providence of my Lord, who knoweth well what is most expedient for me.
Letter 46

FEBRUARY

FEBRUARY 10

The Lord who, in his deep wisdom, turneth about all the wheels and turning of such changes, shall also dispose of that for the best to you and yours.
Letter 46

FEBRUARY 11

God can come over greater mountains than these, we believe, for he worketh his greatest works contrary to carnal reason and means.
Letter 47

FEBRUARY 12

I desire not to go on the lee side or sunny side of religion, or to put truth betwixt me and a storm; my Saviour did not so for me, who in his suffering took the windy side of the hill.
Letter 40

FEBRUARY 13

Send a heavy heart up to Christ, it shall be welcome.
Letter 50

The Lord saw a nail in my heart loose, and he hath now fastened it. Honour be to his majesty.
Letter 46

FEBRUARY 14

You break your heart and grow heavy, and forget that

FEBRUARY

Christ hath your name engraven on the palms of his hand in great letters.
Letter 50

FEBRUARY 15

What is this we are doing, breaking the neck of our faith? We are not come as yet to the mouth of the Red Sea, and howbeit [although] we were, for his honour's sake he must dry it up.
Letter 51

FEBRUARY 16

I charge you in the name of the Son of God, to rest upon your Rock that is higher than yourself.
Letter 52

FEBRUARY 17

Be not cast down. If you saw him who is standing on the shore, holding out his arms to welcome you on land, you would not only wade through a sea of wrongs, but through hell itself to be at him.
Letter 54

FEBRUARY 18

It is a mercy in this stormy sea to get a second wind, for none of the saints get a first. But they must take the winds as the Lord of the seas causeth them to blow, and the inn as the Lord and Master of the inns hath ordered it. If contentment were here, heaven were not heaven.
Letter 56

FEBRUARY

FEBRUARY 19

We live in a sea where many have suffered shipwreck, and have need that Christ sit at the helm of the ship.
Letter 56

FEBRUARY 20

My charge is to you to believe, rejoice, sing and triumph.
Letter 57

FEBRUARY 21

He who forbiddeth to add affliction to affliction, will he do it himself?
Letter 62

FEBRUARY 22

I verily think the chains of my Lord Jesus are all overlaid with pure gold.
Letter 63

FEBRUARY 23

Faith will trust the Lord, and is not hasty nor headstrong.
Letter 63

FEBRUARY 24

Let us help one another with our prayers. ... I think it the Lord's wise love that feeds us with hunger.
Letter 63

FEBRUARY

FEBRUARY 25

I will charge my soul to believe and to wait for him, and will follow his providence, and not go before it, nor stay behind it.
Letter 63

FEBRUARY 26

I know it were necessary to take more pains than we do, and not to make heaven a city more easily taken than God hath made it.
Letter 66

FEBRUARY 27

Howbeit ye get strokes and sour looks from your Lord, yet believe his love more than your own feeling, for this world can take nothing from you that is truly yours, and death can do you no wrong. Your rock doth not ebb and flow, but your sea. That which Christ hath said, he will bide [abide] by it.
Letter 69

FEBRUARY 28

Christ will lippen [entrust] the taking you to heaven neither to yourself nor any deputy, but only to himself.
Letter 69

FEBRUARY 29

I want [lack] both pen and words to set forth the fairness, beauty and sweetness of Christ's love, and the

FEBRUARY

honour of this cross of Christ [tribulation from Christ].
Letter 66

March

MARCH 1

Whoso looketh to the white side of Christ's cross and can take it up handsomely with faith and courage, shall find it such a burden as sails are to a ship or wings to a bird.
Letter 71

MARCH 2

If it were come to exchanging of crosses [tribulations], I would not exchange my cross with any.
Letter 70

MARCH 3

I know his comforts are no dreams. He would not put his seal on blank paper, nor deceive his afflicted ones that trust in him.
Letter 70

MARCH 4

Ye must go in at heaven's gates, and your book in your hand, still learning.
Letter 70

MARCH

MARCH 5

There is a nick [point] in Christianity, to the which whosoever cometh, they see and feel more than others can do.
Letter 70

MARCH 6

God grant that in my temptations I come not on his wrong side again, and never again fall a-raving against my Physician in my fever.
Letter 71

MARCH 7

Water runneth not faster through a sieve than our warnings slip from us.
Letter 72

MARCH 8

Christ's cross [tribulation] is neither a cruel nor unkind mercy, but the love-token of a father.
Letter 72

MARCH 9

I see grace groweth best in winter. ... In my prison he hath shown me daylight.
Letter 74

MARCH

MARCH 10

I have cause now to trust Christ's promise more than his gloom [frown].
Letter 75

MARCH 11

He looketh to what I desire to be, and not to what I am.
Letter 76

MARCH 12

He will see to his own gold, and save that from being consumed with the fire.
Letter 76

MARCH 13

Grace tried is better than grace, and it is more than grace: it is glory in its infancy.
Letter 76

MARCH 14

Living on trust by faith may well content us.
Letter 76

MARCH 15

I know this much of Christ, that he is not ill [hard] to be found, nor lordly of [haughty in] his love.
Letter 79

MARCH

MARCH 16

To pray and believe now, when Christ seems to give you a nay-say [refusal], is more than it was before.
Letter 80

MARCH 17

There is required patience on our part, till the summer-fruit in heaven be ripe for us. It is in the bud, but there be many things to do before our harvest come.
Letter 81

MARCH 18

We love to carry a heaven to heaven with us, and would have two summers in one year, and no less than two heavens. The man Christ got but one only, and shall we have two?
Letter 81

MARCH 19

Stoop! It is a low entry to go in at heaven's gate.
Letter 82

MARCH 20

He is the short cut and the nearest way to an out-gate of [deliverance from] all your burdens. Ye shall be dearly welcome to him.
Letter 82

MARCH

MARCH 21

Oh for a soul as wide as the utmost circle of the highest heaven that containeth all, to contain his love! And yet I could hold little of it.
Letter 82

MARCH 22

Many would follow Christ, but with a reservation that Christ would cry down crosses, and cry up fair weather, and a summer sky and sun, till we were all fairly landed at heaven.
Letter 83

MARCH 23

If we knew ourselves well, to want [lack] temptations is the greatest temptation of all.
Letter 83

MARCH 24

God hath made many fair flowers, but the fairest of them all is heaven, and the flower of all flowers is Christ.
Letter 87

MARCH 25

However it be, I know Christ winneth heaven in despite of hell. ... Christ, with all his little ones under his two wings, and in the compass or circle of his arms, is so sure that, [if you] cast them and him into the ground of the sea, he shall come up again and not lose

MARCH

one. An odd [occasional] one cannot, nor shall, be lost in the telling [counting].
Letter 85

MARCH 26

We would fain stay and spin out a heaven to ourselves, on this side of the water, but sorrow, want [lack], changes, crosses and sin are both woof [weft] and warp in that ill-spun web [fabric].
Letter 87

MARCH 27

Our crosses would not bite upon us if we were heavenly-minded.
Letter 84

God be thanked that Christ in his children can endure a stress and a storm, howbeit soft nature would fall down in pieces.
Letter 85

MARCH 28

Our Lord loppeth the branches off our worldly joys, well nigh the root, on purpose that they should not thrive.
Letter 93

MARCH 29

When we shall come home, and shall look back to pains and suffering, then shall we see life and sorrow to be less than one step or stride from a prison to glo-

MARCH

ry, and that our little inch of time-suffering is not worthy of our first night's welcome home to heaven.
Letter 88

MARCH 30

Wiles will not take us past the cross. It is folly to think to steal [creep] to heaven with a whole skin [unscathed].
Letter 89

MARCH 31

Hold your peace, and stay yourselves upon the Holy One of Israel. Hearken to what he hath said in crossing of [frustrating] your desires; he will speak peace to his people.
Letter 90

April

APRIL 1

Faith's necessity, in a fair day, is never known aright.
Letter 92

APRIL 2

One smile of Christ's face is now to me as a kingdom.
Letter 92

APRIL 3

God send me no more, for my part of paradise, but Christ. And surely I were rich enough, and as well heavened [made partaker of heaven] as the best of them, if Christ were my heaven.
Letter 87

APRIL 4

He hath eased me, when I saw it not, lifting the cross [burden] off my shoulders, so that I think it to be but a feather, because underneath are everlasting arms.
Letter 97

APRIL 5

I know no sweeter way to heaven than through free grace and hard trials together, and one of these cannot well want [lack] another.
Letter 95

APRIL

APRIL 6

I have the company of a Lord who can teach us all to be kind. ... Let him make of me what he pleaseth, if he maketh salvation out of it to me.
Letter 97

APRIL 7

Oh, how ebb [shallow] a soul have I to take in Christ's love!
Letter 94

APRIL 8

Providence is not rolled upon unequal and crooked wheels; all things work together for the good of those who love God, and are called according to his purpose. Ere it be long, we shall see the white side of God's providence.
Letter 98

APRIL 9

Yet believe his love in a patient onwaiting [expectant wait] and believing in the dark. Ye must learn to swim and hold up your head above the water, even when the sense of his presence is not with you to hold up your chin.
Letter 100

APRIL 10

We make an idol of our will. As many lusts in us, as many gods; we are all godmakers [makers of gods].

APRIL

We are like to lose Christ, the true God, in the throng of those new and false gods.
Letter 102

APRIL 11

He was always kind to my soul, but never so kind as now, in my greatest extremities.
Letter 103

APRIL 12

Dig deep, and sweat, and labour, and take pains [great efforts] for him and set by [dedicate] as much time in the day for him as you can. He will be won with labour.
Letter 104

APRIL 13

I thought it had been an easy thing to be a Christian, and that to seek God had been at the next door. But oh the windings, the turnings, the ups and the downs that he hath led me through! And I see yet much way to the ford [a long way to the crossing into heaven].
Letter 104

APRIL 14

It is a mercy that the poor wandering sheep get a dyke-side [lee side of a wall] in this stormy day, and a leaking ship a safe harbour, and a sea-sick passenger a sound and soft bed ashore.
Letter 105

APRIL

APRIL 15

I love Christ's worst reproaches, his glooms, his cross, better than all the world's plastered glory.
Letter 105

APRIL 16

I may be a book-man [a scholarly man], and [yet] be an idiot and stark fool in Christ's way! Learning will not beguile [deceive] Christ.
Letter 106

APRIL 17

I doubt not but more would fetch heaven, if they believed not heaven to be at the next door.
Letter 106

APRIL 18

He delighteth to take up fallen bairns [children], and to mend broken brows.
Letter 107

APRIL 19

He hath taught me to be content with a borrowed fireside and an unco [strange] bed, and I think I have lost nothing, the income is so great.
Letter 111

APRIL 20

His bairns must often have the frosty cold side of the hill, and set down both their bare feet among thorns.

APRIL

His love hath eyes, and, in the meantime, is looking on. ... Hiding of his face is wise love.
Letter 107

APRIL 21

I would not exchange my Lord Jesus with all the comfort out of heaven.
Letter 108

APRIL 22

Salvation is supposed to be at the door, and Christianity is thought an easy task, but I find it hard, and the way straight and narrow, were it not that my Guide is content to wait on [serve] me and to care for a tired traveller.
Letter 109

APRIL 23

I hope to live by faith, and swim without a mass or bundle of joyful sense under my chin—at least to venture, albeit I should be ducked [with my head below water].
Letter 110

APRIL 24

Our pride must have winter weather to rot it.
Letter 107

APRIL

APRIL 25

If twenty crosses [tribulations] be written for you in God's book, they will come to nineteen, and then at last to one, and after that to nothing.
Letter 112

APRIL 26

He taketh the bairns in his arms when they come to a deep water; at least, when they lose ground, and are put to [obliged to] swim, then his hand is under their chin.
Letter 113

APRIL 27

God hath called you to Christ's side, and the wind is now in Christ's face in this land. And seeing ye are with him, ye cannot expect the lee side, or the sunny side of the brae [hill].
Letter 115

APRIL 28

It were better that men would see that their wisdom be holy, and their holiness wise.
Letter 116

APRIL 29

Heaven is not at the next door. I find Christianity to be a hard task.
Letter 124

APRIL

APRIL 30

I hope, when a change cometh, to cast anchor at midnight upon the Rock which he hath taught me to know in this daylight; whither I may run, when I must say my lesson without book, and believe in the dark.
Letter 118

May

MAY 1

He knoweth that I have little but the love of that love, and that I shall be happy, suppose I never get another heaven but only an eternal, lasting feast of that love.
Letter 120

MAY 2

Temptations will come, but if they be not made welcome by you, ye have the best of it. Be jealous over yourself and your own heart, and keep touches with [close to] God.
Letter 121

MAY 3

For worldly things, seeing there are meadows and fair flowers in your way to heaven, a smell in the bygoing [passing] is sufficient. He that would reckon and tell [count] all the stones in his way, in a journey of three or four hundred miles, and write up in his count-book [accounting book] all the herbs and the flowers growing in his way, might come short of his journey. You cannot stay, in your inch of time, to lose your day (seeing that you are in haste, and the night and your afternoon will not bide [await] you), in setting your heart on this vain world.
Letter 122

MAY

MAY 4

It is easy to get good words and a comfortable message from our Lord, even from such rough sergeants as diverse temptations. Thanks to God for crosses!
Letter 122

MAY 5

Let us be faithful, and care for our own part ... and lay Christ's part on himself. Duties are ours, events are the Lord's.
Letter 107

MAY 6

Go where you will, your soul shall not sleep sound but in Christ's bosom.
Letter 127

MAY 7

When Christ in love giveth a blow, it doeth a soul good, and it is a kind of comfort and joy to it to get a cuff with [blow from] the lovely, sweet, and soft hand of Jesus.
Letter 130

MAY 8

What power and strength are in his love! I am persuaded it can climb a steep hill with hell upon its back, and swim through water and not drown, and sing in the fire and find no pain, and triumph in losses, pris-

MAY

ons, sorrows, exile, disgrace, and laugh and rejoice in death.
Letter 130

MAY 9

Our soft nature would be borne through the troubles of this miserable life in Christ's arms, and it is his wisdom, who knoweth our mould, that his bairns go wet-shod and cold-footed to heaven.
Letter 131

MAY 10

A borrowed vision in this life would be my borrowed and begun heaven, whill [till] the long, long, looked-for day dawn.
Letter 130

MAY 11

Think not much of a storm upon the ship that Christ saileth in. There shall no passenger fall overboard, but the crazed [damaged] ship and the seasick passenger shall come to land safe.
Letter 131

MAY 12

When the saints are under trials and well humbled, little sins raise great cries and war-shouts in the conscience, and in prosperity, conscience is a pope, to give dispensations, and let out and in, and give latitude and elbow room to our heart. Oh, how little care we

MAY

for pardon at Christ's hand, when we make dispensations!
Letter 133

MAY 13

It is strange and wonderful, that he would think [it] long [to be] in heaven without us, and that he would have the company of sinners to solace and delight himself withal [with] in heaven.
Letter 133

MAY 14

It were good that we prisoners of hope know of our stronghold to run to, before the storm come on.
Letter 134

MAY 15

Go on through your waters without wearying. Your Guide knoweth the way. Follow him, and cast your cares and temptations upon him … he wearieth not to be kind.
Letter 137

MAY 16

We build castles in the air, and night-dreams are our daily idols that we dote on. Salvation, salvation is our only necessary thing. Call home your thoughts to this work, to enquire for your well-beloved.
Letter 136

MAY

MAY 17

Ye have heard of the patience of Job. When he lay in the ashes, God was with him ... comforting his soul, and he took him up at last. That God is not dead yet; he will stoop and take up fallen bairns.
Letter 138

MAY 18

When I count [account] with him for his mercies to me, I must stand still and wonder, and go away as a poor dyvour [debtor], who hath nothing to pay.
Letter 140

MAY 19

Your Master, Christ, won heaven with strokes [blows]: it is a besieged castle; it must be taken with violence. Oh, this world thinketh heaven but at the next door, and that godliness may sleep in a bed of down till it come to heaven! But that will not do it.
Letter 141

MAY 20

I was swimming in the depths, but Christ had his hand under my chin all the time, and took good heed that I should not lose breath.
Letter 141

MAY

MAY 21

There are infinite plies [folds] in his love, that the saints will never win to unfold [succeed in unfolding].
Letter 152

MAY 22

The devil and the world cannot wound the love of Christ. ... Sufferings blunt not the fiery edge of love. Cast love into the floods of hell, it will swim above.
Letter 143

MAY 23

Let no man scaur [take fright] at Christ's cross, or raise an ill report upon him or it, for he beareth the sufferer and it both.
Letter 144

MAY 24

There is no little thrusting and thronging [pushing] to thrust in at heaven's gates; it is a castle taken by force.
Letter 147

MAY 25

The worst things of Christ—his reproaches, his cross—are better than Egypt's treasures.
Letter 148

MAY

MAY 26

I must give over all attempts to fathom the depth of his love. All I can do is but to stand beside his great love, and look and wonder.
Letter 151

MAY 27

Happy is your soul if Christ man the house, and take the keys himself, and command all.
Letter 142

MAY 28

His mercy hath a set period, and appointed place, how far and no farther the sea of affliction shall flow, and where the waves thereof shall be stayed.
Letter 158

MAY 29

I know now how to shut the lock, and unbolt my well-beloved's door, and he maketh a poor stranger welcome when he cometh to his house.
Letter 155

MAY 30

I find it to be most true, that the greatest temptation out of hell is to live without temptations.
Letter 157

MAY

MAY 31

Faith is the better of the free air, and of the sharp winter storm in its face. Grace withereth without adversity.
Letter 157

June

JUNE 1

The devil is but God's master fencer [swordsman], to teach us to handle our weapons.
Letter 157

JUNE 2

His love hath neither brim nor bottom; his love is like himself, it passeth all natural understanding. I go to fathom it with my arms, but it is as if a child would take the globe of sea and land in his two short arms.
Letter 153

JUNE 3

He, who is afflicted in all your afflictions, looketh not on you in your sad hours with an insensible heart or dry eyes.
Letter 158

JUNE 4

I know that our dearest Lord will pardon and pass by our honest errors and mistakes, when we mind his honour.
Letter 163

JUNE

JUNE 5

Down-casting, sense of guiltiness and hunger are often best for us.
Letter 159

JUNE 6

Learn to believe Christ better than his strokes; himself and his promises better than his glooms.
Letter 161

JUNE 7

When the Lord's blessed will bloweth across your desires, it is best, in humility, to strike sail [show submission] to him.
Letter 161

JUNE 8

The Lord is equal in his ways, but my guiltiness often over-mastereth [overcometh] my believing.
Letter 162

JUNE 9

We forget that as our gifts and light grow, so God's gain and the interest of his talents [the rate of interest on his money] should grow also, and that we cannot pay God with the old use and wont which we gave him seven years ago.
Letter 158

JUNE

JUNE 10

I have no seat for my faith to sit on, but bare omnipotence and God's holy arm and goodwill.
Letter 163

JUNE 11

I must go in at heaven's gates, borrowing strength from Christ.
Letter 165

JUNE 12

Number your talents, and see what you have to render back.
Letter 166

JUNE 13

He is every way higher and deeper and broader than the shallow and ebb [insufficient] handbreadth of my short dim light can take up.
Letter 169

JUNE 14

Oh, let this bit of love of ours, this inch half-span length of heavenly longing, meet with thine infinite love!
Letter 169

JUNE

JUNE 15

If I had no other heaven than a continual hunger for Christ, such a heaven of ever-working hunger were still a heaven to me.
Letter 170

JUNE 16

Be not discouraged at broken and spilled resolutions, but to [go to] it, and to it again.
Letter 173

JUNE 17

Oh how steadable [profitable] a thing is a Saviour, to make a sinner rid of his chains and fetters.
Letter 170

JUNE 18

Every day we may see some new thing in Christ; his love hath neither brim nor bottom.
Letter 171

JUNE 19

It is Christianity, my heart, to be sincere, unfeigned, honest, and upright-hearted before God, and to live and serve God, suppose there was not one man nor woman in all the world dwelling beside you to eye [look at] you. Any little grace that ye have, see that it be sound and true.
Letter 172

JUNE

JUNE 20

Ye must in all things aim at God's honour. Ye must eat, drink, sleep, buy, sell, sit, stand, speak pray, read, and hear the Word, with a heart-purpose that God may be honoured.
Letter 172

JUNE 21

Commit all your ways and actions to God, by prayer, supplication and thanksgiving, and count not much of being mocked, for Christ Jesus was mocked before you.
Letter 172

JUNE 22

When I look to my guiltiness, I see that my salvation is one of our Saviour's greatest miracles, either in heaven or earth.
Letter 170

JUNE 23

Venture to take the wind on your face for Christ.
Letter 174

JUNE 24

A heart of iron, and iron doors, will not hold Christ out.
Letter 175

Let no man think he shall lose at Christ's hands in suf-

JUNE

fering for him.
Letter 176

JUNE 25

I cannot—nay, I would not—be quit of Christ's love. He hath left the mark behind where he gripped. He goeth away and leaveth me and his burning love to wrestle together, and I can scarce win my meat of his love because of his absence.
Letter 176

JUNE 26

Glorify the Lord in your sufferings, and take his banner of love and spread it over you. Others will follow you, if they see you strong in the Lord.
Letter 177

JUNE 27

I know that my Lord can make long, and broad, and high, and deep glory to his name out of this bit feckless [weak] body, for Christ looketh not what stuff he maketh glory out of.
Letter 177

Faith in times past hath stopped a leak in my crazed bark [damaged boat], and half-filled my sails with a fair wind.
Letter 178

JUNE

JUNE 28

I believe that when Christ draweth blood, he hath skill to cut the right vein. I know that Christ is not obliged to let me see both the sides of my cross [burden], and turn it over and over that I may see all.
Letter 178

JUNE 29

I would that I could build as much on this, 'My Christ is God', as it would bear. I might lay all the world upon it.
Letter 178

We might beg ourselves rich (if we were wise) if we could hold out our withered hands to Christ, and learn to suit [entreat] and seek, ask and knock.
Letter 178

JUNE 30

I would not have Christ's love entering into me, but I would enter into it, and be swallowed up of [by] that love.
Letter 178

I hope that my ship shall ride it out, seeing Christ is willing to blow his sweet wind in my sails, and mendeth and closeth the leaks in my ship, and ruleth all. It will be strange if a believing passenger be casten [cast] overboard.
Letter 179

July

JULY 1

Examine yourself if ye be in good earnest in Christ. ... Many think they believe, but never tremble: the devils are farther on than these.
Letter 180

Wrestle for him, and take men's feud for God's favour; there is no comparison betwixt these.
Letter 180

JULY 2

Oh, that people would speer [search] out Christ, and never rest whill they find him.
Letter 180

Sanctified thoughts—thoughts made conscience of and called in and kept in awe—are green fuel that burn not, and are a water for Satan's coal.
Letter 181

JULY 3

His kisses and his visits to his dearest ones are thin sown. He could not let out his rivers of love upon his own, but these rivers would be in hazard of loosening

JULY

a young plant at the root. And he knoweth this of you.
Letter 187

I am sure that while Christ lives, I am well enough friendstead [befriended].
Letter 188

JULY 4

He is a miracle and a world's wonder to a seeking and a weeping sinner, but yet such a miracle as shall be seen by them who will come and see.
Letter 181

We creep in under our Lord's wings in the great shower, and the water cannot come through those wings.
Letter 182

JULY 5

What can ail faith, seeing Christ suffereth himself (with reverence to him be it spoken) to be commanded by it, and Christ commandeth all things?
Letter 182

JULY 6

Thrice blessed, and eternally blessed are they who are out of themselves and above themselves, that they may be in love united to him.
Letter 189

JULY

JULY 7

Lay all your loads and your weights by faith upon Christ; take ease to yourself, and let him bear all. He can, he dow [is able], he will bear you, howbeit hell were upon your back.
Letter 186

JULY 8

If ye love but Christ's sunny side, and would have only summer weather and a land-gate [overland route], not a sea-way [rough sea] to heaven, your profession will play you a slip [fail], and the winter well will go dry again in summer.
Letter 186

JULY 9

If men could do no more, I would have them to wonder. If we cannot be filled with Christ's love, we may be filled with wondering.
Letter 186

Time cannot change him in his love. Ye may yourself ebb and flow, rise and fall, wax and wane, but your Lord is this day as he was yesterday. And it is your comfort that your salvation is not rolled upon wheels of your own making, neither have ye to do with a Christ of your own shaping.
Letter 187

JULY

JULY 10

Faith hath sense of sickness [is conscious of its infirmities] and looketh, like a friend, to the promises—and, looking to Christ therein, is glad to see a known face.
Letter 181

His mercy sendeth always a letter of defiance to all your sins, if there were ten thousand more of them.
Letter 181

JULY 11

God be thanked that our salvation is coasted [brought to the coast], and landed, and shored upon Christ, who is master of winds and storms! And what sea winds can blow the coast or the land out of its place?
Letter 189

JULY 12

Our waters are but ebb [shallow], and come neither to our chin, nor to the stopping of our breath. I may see (if I would borrow eyes from Christ) dry land, and that near [nearby].
Letter 196

JULY 13

I hold my peace, because he hath done it. My shallow and ebb [insufficient] thoughts are not the compass which Christ saileth by. ... For there are windings, and tos and fros, in his ways, which blind bodies [people] like us cannot see.
Letter 183

JULY

JULY 14

As a child cannot hold two apples in his little hand, but the one putteth the other out of its room [place], so neither can we be masters and lords of two loves.
Letter 195

Let us be ready for shipping [departing by ship], against the time [when] our Lord's wind and tide call for us.
Letter 195

JULY 15

Time shall file off, by little and little, our iron bolts [shackles] which are now on legs and arms, and out-date [put out of date] and wear out trouble threadbare and holey [holed], and then wear them to nothing; for what I suffered yesterday, I know, shall never come again to trouble me.
Letter 196

JULY 16

He must go and come, because his infinite wisdom thinketh it best for you. We shall be together one day.
Letter 192

Let us then be wise in our choice, and choose and wale [select] our own blessedness, which is to trust in the Lord.
Letter 192

JULY

JULY 17

Our hope is not hung upon such an untwisted thread as 'I imagine so' or 'it is likely', but the cable, the strong towe [rope] of our fastened anchor, is the oath and promise of him who is eternal verity.
Letter 196

JULY 18

The thing that we mistake is the want [lack] of victory. We hold that to be the mark of one that hath no grace. Nay, say I, the want of *fighting* were a mark of no grace, but I shall not say the want of *victory* is such a mark.
Letter 203

JULY 19

Our salvation is fastened with God's own hand, and with Christ's own strength, to the strong stoup [pillar] of God's unchangeable nature.
Letter 196

JULY 20

Certainly it is a cumbersome thing to keep a foolish child from falls and broken brows, and weeping for this and that toy, and rash running, and sickness and bairns' [children's] diseases. Ere he win [get successfully] through them all, and win out of the mires, he costeth meickle [much] black cumbery and fashery [trouble and bother] to his keepers. And so is a believer a cumbersome [troublesome] piece of work and an

JULY

ill-ravelled hesp [tangled ball of yarn] (as we use to say) to Christ. But God be thanked, for many spilled salvations and many ill-ravelled hesps hath Christ mended since first he entered [became] tutor to lost mankind. Oh, what could we bairns do without him! How soon would we mar all!
Letter 196

JULY 21

Every man blameth the devil for his sins. But the great devil, the house-devil of every man, the house-devil that eateth and lieth in every man's bosom, is that idol that killeth all, *himself*. Oh, blessed are they who can deny themselves, and put Christ in the room of themselves!
Letter 198

JULY 22

It cost Christ and all his followers sharp showers and hot sweats ere they got to the top of the mountain. But still our soft nature would have heaven coming to our bedside when we are sleeping, and lying down with us, that we might go to heaven in warm clothes. But all that came there found wet feet by the way, and sharp storms that did take the hide [skin] off their face, and found tos and fros, and ups and downs, and many enemies by the way.
Letter 198

JULY

JULY 23

My Lord now hath given me experience (howbeit-weak and small) that our best fare here is hunger.
Letter 197

It is good for us that ever Christ took the cumber [burden] of us; it is our heaven to lay many weights and burdens upon Christ, and to make him all we have, root and top, beginning and ending of our salvation.
Letter 196

JULY 24

Oh, if our faith could ride it out against the high and proud waves and winds, when our sea seemeth to be all on fire!
Letter 196

JULY 25

If my fire and the devil's water make crackling like thunder in the air, I am the less feared [afraid]. For where there is fire, it is Christ's part, which I lay and bind upon him, to keep in the coal [prevent the coals falling out of the fire], and to pray the Father that my faith fail not, if I in the meantime be wrestling and doing and fighting and mourning.
Letter 203

JULY 26

Oh that Christ would break down the old narrow vessels of these narrow and ebb [shallow] souls, and make

JULY

fair, deep, wide and broad souls to hold a sea and a full tide (flowing over all its banks) of Christ's love!
Letter 210

JULY 27

Our Lord never getteth so kind a look of us, nor our love in such a degree, nor our faith in such a measure of steadfastness, as he getteth out of the furnace of our tempting fears and sharp trials.
Letter 211

JULY 28

I know that he doth in many seek nothing so much as faith, that can endure summer and winter in their extremity. Faint not—the miles to heaven are but few and short.
Letter 211

JULY 29

His breath is never so hot—his love casteth never such a flame—as when this world, and those who should be the helpers of our joy, cast water on our coal.
Letter 211

JULY 30

I know that it is our sin that we would have sanctification on the sunny side of the hill, and holiness with nothing but summer, and no crosses [tribulations] at all.
Letter 215

JULY

JULY 31

It is the infinite Godhead that must allay the sharpness of your hunger after happiness. Yield to no winds, but ride out, and let Christ be your anchor.
Letter 213

August

AUGUST 1

What further trials are before me, I know not. But I know that Christ will have a saved soul of me over on the other side of the water, on the yonder side of crosses [beyond tribulations], and beyond men's wrongs.
Letter 214

AUGUST 2

No man getteth Christ with ill-will [on Christ's part]; no man cometh and is not welcome. No man cometh and rueth [regrets] his voyage.
Letter 226

AUGUST 3

God be thanked, that this world hath not power to cry us down [defraud us from] so many pounds, as rulers cry down light gold or light silver. We shall stand for as much as our master-coiner, Christ, whose coin, arms, and stamp we bear, will have us. Christ hath no miscarrying [faulty] balance.
Letter 211

AUGUST

AUGUST 4

I see that grace hath a field to play upon and to course up and down in our wants [lacks], so that I am often thanking God, not for guiltiness, but for guiltiness for Christ to whet and sharpen his grace upon. It is a blessed fever that fetcheth Christ to the bedside.
Letter 216

AUGUST 5

I am sure that we are niggards [misers] and sparing bodies [cautious people] in seeking. I verily judge that we know not how much may be had in this life; there is yet something beyond all that we see, that seeking would light upon.
Letter 222

AUGUST 6

It is neither shame nor pride for a drowning man to swim to a rock, nor for a ship-broken [shipwrecked] soul to run himself ashore upon Christ.
Letter 217

It is not pride for a drowning man to grip to the rock. It is your glory to lay hold on your Rock.
Letter 221

AUGUST 7

I find my Lord Jesus cometh not in that precise way that I lay wait for him; he hath a gate [road] of his own.
Letter 222

AUGUST

AUGUST 8

My longest measures are too short for Christ—my depth is ebb [shallow], and the breadth of my affections to Christ narrowed and pinched.
Letter 216

AUGUST 9

Step over this hand-breadth of world's glory into our Lord's new world of grace, and ye will laugh at the feathers that children are chasing in the air.
Letter 224

AUGUST 10

Every man is a believer in daylight: a fair day seemeth to be made all of faith and hope.
Letter 223

AUGUST 11

Our crosses [tribulations] will never draw blood of the joy of the Holy Ghost and peace of conscience. Strive to thring [press] through the thorns of this life to be at Christ.
Letter 226

AUGUST 12

If ye will be content to take heaven by violence, and the wind on your face for Christ and his cross, I am here one who hath some trial of Christ's cross, and I can say that Christ was ever kind to me. But he over-

AUGUST

cometh himself [he excelleth] (if I may speak so) in kindness while I suffer for him.
Letter 225

AUGUST 13

If I have any love to him, Christ hath both love to me, and wit [aptitude] to guide his love.
Letter 215

AUGUST 14

Wants [lacks] are my best riches, because I have these supplied by Christ.
Letter 222

AUGUST 15

I know my Lord is no niggard [miser]: he can—and it becometh him well—to give more than my narrow soul can receive.... Christ is a well of life, but who knoweth how deep it is to the bottom?
Letter 226

AUGUST 16

There is not such breadth and elbow-room in the way to heaven as men believe.
Letter 227

AUGUST 17

This blind world seeth not that sufferings are Christ's armour, wherein he is victorious.
Letter 228

AUGUST

Ye are an arrow of his own making. Let him shoot you against a wall of brass; your point [arrow point] shall keep whole.
Letter 229

AUGUST 18

It is good that your crosses [tribulations] will but convoy you to heaven's gates—in they cannot go; the gates shall be closed upon them when ye shall be admitted to the throne.
Letter 230

AUGUST 19

Take what way we can to heaven, the way is hedged up with crosses; there is no way but to break through them. Wit and wiles, shifts and laws, will not find out a way round the cross of Christ, but we must through [go through the cross].
Letter 237

AUGUST 20

Grace, grace, free grace, the merits of Christ for nothing, white and fair, and large Saviour-mercy ... have been and must be the rock that we drowned souls must swim to.
Letter 233

AUGUST 21

I know certainly that my Lord Jesus will not mar nor spill my sufferings; he hath use for them in his house.
Letter 230

AUGUST

AUGUST 22

One thing, by experience, my Lord hath taught me, that the waters betwixt this and heaven may all be ridden, if we be well horsed [mounted]—I mean, if we be in Christ—and not one shall drown by the way, but such as love their own destruction.
Letter 237

AUGUST 23

Set your face to heaven, and make you a stoop [stoop down] at all the low entries in the way, that ye may receive the kingdom as a child.
Letter 237

AUGUST 24

I exhort you not to lose breath, nor to faint in your journey. Your Lord Jesus did sweat and pant ere he got up that mount—he was at 'Father, save me!' with it. I am sure ye love the way better that [because] his holy feet trod it before you.
Letter 238

AUGUST 25

I never knew Christ to ebb or flow, wax or wane. His winds turn not. When he seemeth to change, it is but we who turn our wrong side to him.
Letter 240

AUGUST

AUGUST 26

Crosses [tribulations] are proclaimed as common accidents [providential occurrences] to all the saints, and in them standeth a part of our communion with Christ. But there lieth a sweet casualty [relationship] to the cross, even Christ's presence and his comforts, when they are sanctified.
Letter 240

AUGUST 27

Christ and his cross are not separable in this life. Howbeit, Christ and his cross part at heaven's door, for there is no house-room for crosses [tribulations] in heaven.
Letter 242

AUGUST 28

One tear, one sigh, one sad heart, one fear, one loss, one thought of trouble, cannot find lodging there [in heaven]. They are but the marks of our Lord Jesus down in this wide inn and stormy country, on this side of death.
Letter 242

AUGUST 29

I find that his sweet presence eateth out the bitterness of sorrow and suffering. I think it a sweet thing that Christ saith of my cross, 'Half mine', and that he divideth these sufferings with me, and taketh the larger

AUGUST

share to himself—nay, that I and my whole cross are wholly Christ's.
Letter 242

AUGUST 30

Having him, though my cross were as heavy as ten mountains of iron, when he putteth his sweet shoulder under me and it, my cross is but a feather.
Letter 247

AUGUST 31

When I lose breath climbing up the mountain, he maketh new breath.
Letter 247

September

SEPTEMBER 1

See that Christ lay [would lay] the ground-stone [foundation-stone] of your profession, for wind and rain and spates will not wash away his building. His works have no shorter date than to stand for evermore.
Letter 248

SEPTEMBER 2

Christ taketh as poor men may give. Where there is a mean portion, he is content with the less, if there be sincerity; broken sums, and little, feckless [weak] obedience will be pardoned, and hold the foot [continue the march] with him.
Letter 249

SEPTEMBER 3

I rue not that I made Christ my wale [selection] and my choice; I think him aye [always] the longer the better.
Letter 258

SEPTEMBER 4

It is good, ere the storm rise, to make ready all [everything] and to be prepared to go to the camp [battle-

SEPTEMBER

field] with Christ, seeing he will not keep the house nor sit at the fireside with couchers [cowards].
Letter 251

SEPTEMBER 5

Venture through the thick of all things after Christ, and lose not your Master, Christ, in the throng of this great market.
Letter 252

SEPTEMBER 6

Christ keepeth tryst [appointment] in the fire and water with his own, and cometh ere our breath go out and ere our blood grow cold.
Letter 253

SEPTEMBER 7

Whatever your guiltiness be, yet, when it falleth into the sea of God's mercy, it is but like a drop of blood fallen into the great ocean.
Letter 256

SEPTEMBER 8

I believe through a cloud that sorrow (which hath no eyes) hath but put a veil on Christ's love.
Letter 256

SEPTEMBER 9

God is true in the least, as well as in the greatest, and he must be so to you. Ye must not call him true in the

SEPTEMBER

one page of the leaf and false in the other, for our Lord, in all his writings, never contradicted himself yet.
Letter 249

SEPTEMBER 10

If we could be faithful, our tackling shall not loose [get loose], or our mast break, or our sails blow into the sea.
Letter 260

SEPTEMBER 11

It is not a smooth and easy way, neither will your weather be fair and pleasant. But whatsoever hath seen the invisible God and the fair city makes no reckoning of losses or crosses [tribulations].
Letter 261

SEPTEMBER 12

Let Christ have a commanding power and a king's throne in you.
Letter 262

SEPTEMBER 13

Take Christ, howbeit a storm follow [may follow] him.
Letter 264

SEPTEMBER

SEPTEMBER 14

Our sufferings are washen [washed] in Christ's blood, as well as our souls, for Christ's merits brought a blessing to the crosses [tribulations] of the sons of God.
Letter 265

SEPTEMBER 15

The world knoweth not our life; it is a mystery to them. We have the sunny side of the world and our paradise is far above theirs. Yea, our weeping is above their laughing, which is but like the crackling of thorns under a pot.
Letter 274

SEPTEMBER 16

Know that ye are as near heaven as ye are far from yourself.
Letter 272

SEPTEMBER 17

I am sure that troubles have no prevailing right over us, if they be but our Lord's sergeants to keep us in his ward [custody] while we are on this side of heaven.
Letter 273

SEPTEMBER 18

Your ship shall ride against all storms, if withal [in addition] your anchor be fastened on good ground—I mean within the veil.
Letter 271

SEPTEMBER

SEPTEMBER 19

I pray God that I may not be so ill friendstead [badly befriended] as that Christ my Lord should leave me to be my own tutor and my own physician. Shall I not think that my Lord Jesus, who deserveth his own place very well, will take his own place upon him as it becometh him, and that he will fill his own chair?
Letter 275

SEPTEMBER 20

Howbeit my faith hang by a small tack [temporary stitch] and thread, I hope that the tack shall not break. And howbeit my Lord got no service of me but broken wishes, yet I trust that those will be accepted upon Christ's account.
Letter 275

SEPTEMBER 21

Our Lord's love is not so cruel as to let a poor man see Christ and heaven, and never give him more for want [lack] of money to buy. ... Christ's love is ready to make and provide a ransom, and money for a poor body [person] who hath lost his purse.
Letter 275

SEPTEMBER 22

Misbelief can spin out a hell of heavy and desponding thoughts. Then Christ seeketh law-borrows of [securities from] my unbelieving apprehensions, and chargeth me to believe his daylight at midnight.
Letter 275

SEPTEMBER

SEPTEMBER 23

I see that we must be off our feet in wading a deep water, and then Christ's love findeth timeous [timely] employment at such a dead-lift [deadweight] as that.
Letter 275

SEPTEMBER 24

Ye will not get leave to steal quietly to heaven in Christ's company without a conflict and a cross.
Letter 275

SEPTEMBER 25

A misty dew will stand [suffice] for rain, and do some good, and keep some greenness in the herbs, till our Lord's clouds rue [drizzle] upon the earth and send down a watering of rain. Truly I think Christ's misty dew a welcome message from heaven till my Lord's rain fall.
Letter 277

SEPTEMBER 26

The sea is out, the wind of his Spirit calm, and I cannot buy a wind or, by requesting the sea, cause it to flow again. Only I wait on upon the banks and shoreside till the Lord send a full sea, that with upsails [sails hoisted] I may lift up Christ.
Letter 277

SEPTEMBER

SEPTEMBER 27

Well were [would be] my soul if Christ were the element (mine own element) and that I loved and breathed in him, and if I could not live without him.
Letter 277

SEPTEMBER 28

No man's emptiness and want [lack] layeth an inhibition upon Christ, or hindereth his salvation. And that is far best for me.
Letter 277

SEPTEMBER 29

He hath broken in upon the poor prisoner's soul, like the swelling of Jordan. I am bank and brimful [I am satiated]; a great, high spring-tide of the consolations of Christ have overflowed me.
Letter 289

SEPTEMBER 30

Consider, it is impossible that your idol-sins and ye can go to heaven together—and that they, who will not part with these, can indeed love Christ at the bottom [basically] but only in word and show, which will not do the business.
Letter 280

October

OCTOBER 1

We are still ill [bad] scholars, and will go in at heaven's gates wanting [lacking] the half of our lesson, and shall still be bairns, so long as we are under time's hands and till eternity cause a sun to arise in our souls that shall give us wit [wisdom].
Letter 282

OCTOBER 2

If we were tutors and stewards and masters and lord-carvers [master-carvers] of Christ's love, we should be more lean and worse fed than we are. Our meat doeth us the more good, that [because] Christ keepeth the keys.
Letter 282

OCTOBER 3

Alas, we do not harden our faces against the cold north storms which blow upon Christ's fair face!
Letter 284

OCTOBER 4

It is the Lord's kindness that he will take the scum [dross from melted metal] off us in the fire. Who knoweth how needful winnowing is to us, and what

OCTOBER

dross we must want [be free from] ere we enter into the kingdom of God?
Letter 282

OCTOBER 5

What fools are we in the taking up of him and of his dealing! He hath a gate [way] of his own beyond the thoughts of men, that no foot hath skill to follow him.
Letter 282

OCTOBER 6

Remember how swiftly God's post [express-messenger] time flieth away, and that your forenoon is already spent. Your afternoon will come, and then your evening, and at last night, when ye cannot see to work. Let your heart be set upon finishing of your journey, and summing [adding up] and laying [reckoning] your accounts with your Lord. Oh, how blessed shall ye be to have a joyful welcome of [from] your Lord at night!
Letter 280

OCTOBER 7

We may see how we spill and mar our own fair heaven and our salvation, and how Christ is every day putting in one bone or other (in these fallen souls of ours) in the right place again—and that on this side of the New Jerusalem we shall still have need of forgiving and healing grace.
Letter 282

OCTOBER

OCTOBER 8

So narrow is the entry to heaven, that our knots, our bunches and lumps of pride, and self-love and idol-love and world-love must be hammered off us, that we may thring [push] in, stooping low and creeping through that narrow and thorny entry.
Letter 282

OCTOBER 9

We love well summer-religion, and to be that which sin has made us, even as thin-skinned as if we were made of white paper—and would fain be carried to heaven in a close covered chariot, wishing from our hearts that Christ would give us surety and his hand-write [signature] and his seal (or nothing but a fair summer) until we be landed in at heaven's gates!
Letter 284

OCTOBER 10

We found Christ without a wet foot, and he and his gospel came upon small charges [by free grace] to our doors. But now we must wet our feet to seek him.
Letter 284

OCTOBER 11

Many take but half a grip of Christ, and the wind bloweth them and Christ asunder.
Letter 284

OCTOBER

OCTOBER 12

All of us know the way to a whole skin. And the singlest [most ingenuous] heart that is hath a by-purse [side purse] that will contain the denial of Christ and a fearful backsliding. Oh, how rare a thing it is to be loyal and honest to Christ, when he hath a controversy with the shields of the earth!
Letter 284

OCTOBER 13

We have need to be redeemed from ourselves, rather than from the devil and the world! Learn to put out yourselves, and to put in Christ for yourselves.
Letter 284

OCTOBER 14

He can make one web [woven fabric] of contraries.
Letter 287

OCTOBER 15

If our sinful weakness swell up to the clouds, Christ's strength will swell up to the sun, and far above the heaven of heavens.
Letter 286

OCTOBER 16

Sick children get of [get] Christ's pleasant things to play them withal [to amuse themselves with], because Jesus is most tender of [towards] the sufferer, for he

OCTOBER

was a sufferer himself.
Letter 286

OCTOBER 17

I fear not that too great spates of love wash away the growing corn and loose [loosen] my plants at the roots. Christ doeth no skaith [harm] where he cometh.
Letter 285

OCTOBER 18

Each one knoweth not what a life Christ's love is. Scaur not at [Do not be afraid of] suffering for Christ, for Christ hath a chair and a cushion, and sweet peace for a sufferer.
Letter 285

OCTOBER 19

Because we dow [can] not pay the old, we may not refuse to take on Christ's new debt of mercy...For my part, let me stand for evermore in his book as a forlorn dyvour [destroyed debtor].
Letter 285

OCTOBER 20

It pleaseth that Spirit of Jesus to blow his sweet wind through a piece of dry stick, that the empty reed may keep no glory to itself.
Letter 286

OCTOBER

OCTOBER 21

Who can find in their heart to sin against love—and such a love as the glorified in heaven shall delight to dive into, and drink of forever?
Letter 288

OCTOBER 22

Christ and his truth will not divide, and his truth hath not latitude and breadth, that ye may take some of it and leave other some of it. Nay, the gospel is like a small hair, that hath no breadth, and will not cleave [split] in two.
Letter 204

OCTOBER 23

And howbeit we cannot attain to this denial of me and mine, that we can say, 'I am not myself, myself is not myself, mine own is no longer mine own,' yet our aiming at this in all we do shall be accepted.
Letter 284

OCTOBER 24

Our honest sorrow and sincere aims, together with Christ's intercession, pleading that God would welcome that which we have and forgive what we have not, must be our life till we be over the bound-road [frontier] and in the other country, where the law will get a perfect soul.
Letter 286

OCTOBER

OCTOBER 25

If ye mind [intend] to walk to heaven without a cramp or a crook [trouble], I fear that ye must go your lone [by yourself]. He knoweth our dross and defects, and sweet Jesus pitieth us when weakness and deadness in our obedience is our cross [tribulation] and not our darling.
Letter 286

OCTOBER 26

Believe under a cloud, and wait for him when there is no moonlight nor starlight.
Letter 291

Faith's eyes, that can see through a millstone, can see through a gloom [frown] of God, and under it read God's thoughts of love and peace. Hold fast Christ in the dark.
Letter 291

OCTOBER 27

I know that honest beginnings are nourished by him, even by lovely Jesus, who never yet put out a poor man's dim candle, that [who] is wrestling betwixt light and darkness.
Letter 286

OCTOBER 28

It is a broad river that faith will not look over; it is a mighty and a broad sea, that they of a lively hope cannot behold the furthest bank and other shore thereof.

OCTOBER

Look over the water—your anchor is fixed within the veil.
Letter 291

OCTOBER 29

Let your faith frist [credit] God a little, and not be afraid for a smoking firebrand. ... Your faith is a free lord, and cannot be a captive.
Letter 291

OCTOBER 30

False under-water [filthy bilge water], not seen, is dangerous, and that is a leak and rift in the bottom of an enlightened conscience, often falling and sinning against light.
Letter 284

OCTOBER 31

Let my broken words go up to heaven. When they come up into the great Angel's golden censer, that compassionate Advocate will put together my broken prayers, and perfume them. Words are but the accidents of [*i.e.*, not of the essential nature of] prayer.
Letter 293

November

NOVEMBER 1

If hope can trust Christ, I know that he can and will pay. He hath in heaven the keys of your prison, and can set you at liberty when he pleaseth.
Letter 292

NOVEMBER 2

When my faith was asleep, Christ was awake, and now when I am awake I say, 'He did all things well.'
Letter 294

NOVEMBER 3

Honest sighing is faith breathing and whispering him in the ear. The life is not out of [has not left] faith where there is sighing, looking up with the eyes, and breathing toward God. Hide not thine ear at my breathing (Lamentations 3:56).
Letter 293

NOVEMBER 4

Put on his own mask upon his face, and not your veil made of unbelief, which speaketh as if he borrowed love to you, from you and your demerits and sinful deservings. Oh, no! Christ is man, but he is not like man. He hath man's love in heaven, but it is lustred

NOVEMBER

[made glorious] with God's love, and it is very [true] God's love ye have to do with. When your wheels go about [around], he standeth still. Let God be God.
Letter 295

NOVEMBER 5

Let the Lord absolutely have the ordering of your evils and troubles, and put them off you by recommending your cross [tribulation] and your furnace to him who hath skill to melt his own metal, and knoweth well what to do with his furnace.
Letter 295

NOVEMBER 6

See that Christ be the ground-stone [foundation-stone] of your profession. The sore wind and rain will not wash away his building—his work hath no less date than to stand for evermore.
Letter 304

NOVEMBER 7

When he hath led you through this water that was in your way to glory, there are fewer behind.
Letter 302

NOVEMBER 8

The glory of laying strength upon one that is mighty to save is more than we can think. That piece of service, believing in a smiting Redeemer, is a precious part of obedience.
Letter 299

NOVEMBER

NOVEMBER 9

Christ hath borne the whole complete cross, and … his saints bear but bits and chips—as the apostle saith, 'the remnants' or 'leavings' of the cross (Colossians 1:24).
Letter 323

NOVEMBER 10

The Good Husbandman may pluck his roses and gather in his lilies at midsummer, and, for aught I dare say, in the beginning of the first summer month. And he may transplant young trees out of the lower ground to the higher, where they may have more of the sun and a more free air at any season of the year. What is that to you or me? The goods are his own.
Letter 310

NOVEMBER 11

Hear the rod what it preacheth, and see the name of God (Micah 6:9), and know that there is somewhat of God and heaven in the rod. The majesty of the unsearchable and bottomless ways and judgments of God is not seen in the rod, and the seeing of them requireth the eyes of the man of wisdom. … But he can do no wrong. He cannot halt [stumble]; his goings are equal [his ways are just] who hath done it.
Letter 311

NOVEMBER 12

He numbereth the drops of rain, and knoweth the stars by their names. It would take us much studying

NOVEMBER

to give a name to every star in the firmament, great or small.
Letter 311

NOVEMBER 13

What is Christ's gain is not your loss. Let not that, which is his holy and wise will, be your unbelieving sorrow.
Letter 314

NOVEMBER 14

Let us not weary—the miles to that land are fewer and shorter than when we first believed.
Letter 318

NOVEMBER 15

If Christ pass [sends] his word to wash a sinner, it is less to him than a word to make fair angels of black devils.
Letter 319

NOVEMBER 16

He lieth not in wait for your falls, except it be to take you up.
Letter 320

NOVEMBER 17

A cross of our own choosing, honeyed and sugared with consolations, we cannot have.
Letter 322

NOVEMBER

NOVEMBER 18

That gospel cannot sink—it will make you free, and bear [carry] you out. Christ, the subject of it, is the chosen of God.
Letter 322

NOVEMBER 19

Your guide is good company and knoweth all the miles and the ups and downs in the way.
Letter 324

NOVEMBER 20

He hath taken up your lodging for you.
Letter 321

Rubs [troubles] in the way, where the lodging is so good, are not much.
Letter 323

NOVEMBER 21

I am confident that he will not leave you till he crown the work begun in you.
Letter 308

NOVEMBER 22

Let Christ tutor you as he thinketh good. Ye cannot be marred nor miscarry [come to harm] in his hand.
Letter 324

NOVEMBER

NOVEMBER 23

Ye are Christ's debtor for all providences ... even in that he buildeth an hedge of thorns in your way, for so ye see that his gracious intention is to save you, whether ye will or not.
Letter 326

NOVEMBER 24

Make not haste unbelievingly, but in hope and silence keep the watchtower and look out.
Letter 328

NOVEMBER 25

Christ cannot mistake you; men may. And the calculation and esteem of free grace maketh you to be what you are.
Letter 334

NOVEMBER 26

We fools would have a cross of our own choosing, and would have our gall and wormwood sugared, our fire cold, and our death and grave warmed with heat of life. But he who hath brought many children to glory and lost none is our best tutor.
Letter 332

NOVEMBER 27

Oh, for grace to suffer Christ to tutor his own minors and young heirs! But we cannot endure to be under

NOVEMBER

the actings of his government—we love too much to be our own.
Letter 333

NOVEMBER 28

In the way of duty, and in the silence of faith, go on!
Letter 331

NOVEMBER 29

Stumble not! Men are but men, and God appeareth more and more to be God, and Christ is still Christ.
Letter 335

NOVEMBER 30

I care for nothing, if so be that I were nearer to him. And yet he fleeth not from me. I flee from him, but he pursueth.
Letter 335

December

DECEMBER 1

Although the inhabitants of that land agree in one [unanimously] to sing the song of the Lamb's praise and commendation, so it is here away [in this life], and here only, we have occasion to endure shame and contradiction for his worthy sake.
Letter 336

DECEMBER 2

It is in effect, then, far more honourable to seek conformity to Christ in his cross than to precipitate [halt] in desiring to be like him in glory, and despise and fly away from his sufferings. We use to say [repeatedly say] they are very evil-worthy [unworthy] of the sweet, who will not endure the sour.
Letter 336

DECEMBER 3

It is good that it is not in our power to blast and undo his breathings—his wind bloweth where he listeth.
Letter 342

DECEMBER 4

You have given a testimony for your master; you shall get a meeting when he comes in the clouds.
Letter 337

DECEMBER

DECEMBER 5

As it is the mark of Christ's sheep that they will hear his voice and will not acknowledge a stranger, so it is the mark of faith that it will only receive orders from heaven.
Letter 336

DECEMBER 6

There is a great and wide difference between a name of godliness and the power of godliness. That [that godliness] is hottest when there are fewest witnesses.
Letter 339

DECEMBER 7

Could we but lean, and cast a quiet spirit under the dewings and showerings of him that every moment watereth his vineyard, how happy and blessed were we!
Letter 342

DECEMBER 8

Oh, how little a portion of God do we see! How little study we God! How rarely read we God, or are versed in the lively apprehensions of that great unknown All in All, the glorious Godhead, and the Godhead revealed in Christ! We dwell far from the well, and complain but dryly of our dryness and dullness. We are rather dry than thirsty.
Letter 342

DECEMBER

DECEMBER 9

The Forerunner, who hath landed first, must help to bring the sea-beaten vessel safe to the port, and the sick passengers (who are following the Forerunner) safe ashore.
Letter 345

DECEMBER 10

We make haste; we believe not. Let the only wise God alone; he steereth well.
Letter 354

DECEMBER 11

Oh, if I could adore him in his hidden ways, when there is darkness under his feet and darkness in his pavilion, and clouds are about his throne!
Letter 354

DECEMBER 12

Angels, men, Zion's elders, eye us. But what of all these? Christ is by us, and looketh on us, and writeth up all. Let us pray more, and look less to men.
Letter 357

DECEMBER 13

If so it seem good to him, follow your Forerunner and Guide. It is an unknown land to you, who were never there before. But the land is good, and the company

DECEMBER

before the throne desirable, and he who sitteth on the throne is his lone [is alone] a sufficient heaven.
Letter 351

DECEMBER 14

The cloud will over [pass], could we [if we could] live by faith.
Letter 352

The trembling believer shall not be confounded.
Letter 353

DECEMBER 15

How can we be enlightened when we turn our back on the sun? And must we not be withered when we leave the fountain?
Letter 353

DECEMBER 16

He draweth straight lines, though we think and say they are crooked.
Letter 354

DECEMBER 17

Hoping, believing, patient praying is our life. He loseth no time.
Letter 354

DECEMBER

DECEMBER 18

It would be wisdom, and afford us much sweet peace, if oppressors were looked on as passive instruments, like the saw or axe in the carpenter's hand.
Letter 347

DECEMBER 19

The more ye want [lack], and the more your joy hath run on, the more is owing to you by the promise of grace.
Letter 345

DECEMBER 20

Sure we sin in putting the book in his hand, as if we could teach the Almighty knowledge.
Letter 354

DECEMBER 21

Only by living by faith, and by fetching strength and comfort from Christ, can you be victorious and have right to the precious promises of 'the tree of life', of 'the hidden manna', of the gifted 'morning star' and the like, made to those who overcome.
Letter 359

DECEMBER 22

We count one way, and the Lord counteth another way. He is infallible, and the only wise God, and needeth none of us.
Letter 351

DECEMBER

DECEMBER 23

A duty can never give an offence to Christ, and so none to men.
Letter 359

DECEMBER 24

Fear not ye! Ye are not—ye shall not be— alone: the Father is with you.
Letter 357

DECEMBER 25

It is the art and the skill of faith to read what the Lord writes upon the cross [tribulation], and to spell and construct right his sense.
Letter 361

DECEMBER 26

Could we be from [be brought from] under deadness, and watch unto wrestling and prayer with the Lord, and live more by faith, we should be more than conquerors. Wait upon the Lord! Faint not!
Letter 360

DECEMBER 27

There is a bad way of willful swallowing of a temptation, and not digesting it, or laying it out of [expelling it from] memory without any victoriousness of faith. The Lord, who forbiddeth fainting, forbiddeth also despising.
Letter 361

DECEMBER

DECEMBER 28

Your safest way will be to be silent, and command the heart to utter no repining and fretting thoughts of the holy dispensation of God.
Letter 361

DECEMBER 29

It is not safe to be at pulling and drawing with the omnipotent Lord. Let the pull go with him, for he is strong, and say, 'Thy will be done on earth, as it is in heaven.'
Letter 361

DECEMBER 30

Those that keep the word of his (not their own) patience, shall be delivered from the hour of temptation that shall come on all the earth to try them.
Letter 364

DECEMBER 31

Home! And stay not [do not stop], for the sun is fallen low and nigh the tops of the mountains, and the shadows are stretched out in great length. Linger not by the way! The world and sin would train [entice] you on and make you turn aside. Leave not the way for them, and the Lord Jesus be at the voyage!
Letter 30

www.ingramcontent.com/pod-product-compliance
Lightning Source LLC
Chambersburg PA
CBHW071310040426
42444CB00009B/1961